INDIVIDUA L

DIFFEREN

CE

Unravelling The Human Complexities Of Uniqueness

Dr Sebastian Wayne

CONTENTS

Introduction

In the intricate material of humanity, individual differences form the rich tapestry of human experience. Like threads of varied hues and textures, these differences interweave to create a numerous and fascinating portrait of uniqueness. Through the exploration of man or woman differences, we unravel the complexities of the human condition, gaining perception into the multifaceted nature of identity, behaviour, and cognition. This tapestry of individuality now not solely showcases the tremendous array of human expressions however additionally serves as a testimony to the inherent splendor and complexity of our species. Join us on a journey as we delve into the intricacies of person differences, searching for to understand and respect the numerous mosaic that is humanity.

CHAPTER 1

Introduction

Individual differences refer to the awesome editions among human beings in their psychological traits, behaviours, and organic attributes. Individual difference also refers to the personal psychology that every human being is developing: every human is unique and the psychology he or she is creating will decide his or her lifestyles outcome. Broadly speaking, a person's options have a tendency toward both integrity or infidelity respecting the-objective-truth. Integrity is the exercise of lessening errors by means of being aware, doing the work to apprehend the moment, and rejecting false judgement. Cultures incorrect the man or woman with the aid of inculcating the pursuit of higher authority: something government is or Whatever-God-Is. Some lucky humans receive their individual human power, energy, and authority (HIPEA) to increase integrity rather than infidelity. Michael Polanyi, in his book "Personal Knowledge," 1958, claims, in my paraphrase, that collaboration to discover the-objective-truth and worshipping the Christian God are equivalent practices of HIPEA. I think Polanyi did no longer leave to Whatever-God-Is the freedom to admire discovery greater than to worship. For all I know, Polanyi has it correct, and for all I know, Polanyi and I specific the equal pursuit with character difference. I doubt it, however don't know. This thinking is central to the subject of psychology and related disciplines, acknowledging that each and every character is special owing to a combination of factors along with genetic makeup, environment, experiences, and non-public choices. Individual variations are the psychological characteristics that distinguish one person from another and determine each person's individuality. They are observable when a crew is observed besides the cognizance of the participants of that group that they are being observed, and affect the way and diploma to which individuals will react to specific stimuli. The question of character difference and neighbourhood wishes has a long history in America. There is a social and cultural context in which man or woman variations can be understood. The social fabric in which the individual exists is equally important. Those who have, in the past, encouraged individualism presume that humans will take part in civic responsibilities. But a belief that "freedom" of the man or woman is paramount is regularly understood as greater necessary than differences between individuals or the large community. Popular tradition and popular media extol freedom of the individual but paradoxically, praise these who sacrifice themselves for others (e.g. the soldier, athlete or health service worker who places others first, before merchandising their very own accomplishments. Some of this mindset can be traced to John Stuart Mill who endorsed that "short of harming some other person, each man or woman be accorded total freedom to do as he [or she] wishes". In different words, "self - actualization" is greater essential than any form of self-control that curtails individual freedom. Mill criticized social constraints even though he presupposed that humans had an inherent ethical code to restriction their excesses. Unfortunately, when one abandons moral and moral constraints that locations emphasis on caring for other people or the larger community, the end result can be extreme types of egoism and self-preoccupation. Tradition, custom and social convention end up criticized as limiting the individual in their quest for freedom and happiness. Stress and anxiety are viewed as triggered by means of limitations placed on oneself instead than the stipulations that can be ameliorated by way of devoting extra time to buddies or community efforts that benefit others. Feeling confined via the friends or community one is section of is portrayed as limiting one's very own happiness.

But every other way of perception the paradox of man or woman variations and community cohesion is to view "freedom" as based on virtue ethics (ie virtuous action). Unrestrained freedom can result in positive "evils" (degrees of egotism) inherent in man. Finding a stability between the quest for freedom and happiness as in contrast to civic responsibilities and individual variations is necessary. The alternative is to go to extremes that are damaging to one's spiritual and psychological health. As Edmund Burke noted: "extremes are negative both to advantage and enjoyment". To search for heightened experiences can end result in temporary excitement which is on occasion observed in individual effort (eg competing to be satisfactory in a sport) but these are passing phases and the trip is seldom sustained for any size of time. Failing that, human beings may additionally inn to tablets or opiates to free the thought from anxiety, guilt or shame. Societies are unable to exist barring civility and a sense of neighbourhood which requires self-sacrifice. Such self-sacrifice regularly gives a feel of freedom and happiness, which is extra sustainable. There is a exceptional line between obligations to society and responsibilities to one's man or woman freedom but this state of thought have to be located by means of each person. Going too far in one severe or the other is self-defeating. The Greek philosophers spoke of the cardinal virtues as being "prudence, fortitude, temperance and justice" and placed "moderation" in all matters as one of the chief virtues. To see character variations in terms of "moderation" and temperance and justice can gain a kingdom of well-being. Key aspects influencing man or woman differences include personality traits, intelligence, studying styles, emotional reactivity, and resilience, amongst others. These variations are evident in how people identify the world, interact with others, cope with challenges, and pursue their goals. Understanding individual differences is critical for tailoring academic programs, therapeutic interventions, and workplace practices to higher suit various desires and potentials.

No Individual Is Exactly The Same

The phrase "No Individual A Exactly The Same" underscores a vital factor of human identity and diversity. This in fact ability that each and every character is unique, with no two men and women being exactly alike in each and every aspect. This uniqueness can be attributed to a plethora of factors that outline us as individuals. Let's smash down this concept into its core components to understand it better:

1. Genetic Diversity: At the most basic organic level, each man or woman has a unique set of DNA. Even identical twins,

who share the same genetic makeup, can exhibit differences due to adjustments in gene expression over time and environmental interactions.

2. Experiences: Each character goes via a awesome set of experiences from birth until death. These experiences structure perspectives, have an impact on decisions, and mould personalities uniquely. Even siblings raised in the equal surroundings can interpret and respond to their experiences very differently.

3. Cultural Background: The cultural environment where an character grows up plays a massive position in shaping their beliefs, values, and behaviours. Even within the identical cultural background,

variations such as subcultures, family traditions, and personal interpretations contribute to diversity.

4. Personal Choices: Individuals make several alternatives at some point of their lives, from career paths and pursuits to friends and life partners. These alternatives are influenced through private preferences, ambitions, fears, and desires, all of which add layers to an individual's uniqueness.

5. Psychological Makeup: People fluctuate in their psychological attributes, including character traits, intelligence, emotional responses, and coping mechanisms. These differences are influenced by way of a mixture of genetic factors, upbringing, and

person experiences.

6. Physical Attributes: Apart from genetics dictating physical characteristics, man or woman lifestyles additionally influence aspects like fitness, health, and appearance. Personal choices in fashion, grooming, and physique changes similarly accentuate individuality.

This range is now not simply a human characteristic but a precept of life, reflecting the complexity and richness of existence. It challenges us to recognize and admire the intrinsic value of every individual, fostering empathy, inclusion, and grasp in our interactions. No be counted how comparable two humans would possibly seem, their journeys, perceptions, and essences hold singular stories, making every person an irreplaceable mosaic of the human experience.

Recognizing and valuing individual distinctiveness deepens our understanding of others. Here's how perception this thinking can decorate your standpoint and relationships:

1. Fosters Empathy: Understanding that absolutely everyone has a unique set of experiences and views allows us to approach others with empathy. Realizing that people's reactions and behaviours are shaped via their individual journeys encourages us to meet them with compassion and empathy rather than

judgment.

2.   Encourages   Open-mindedness:
Appreciating forte opens us up to the
substantial range of human experiences
and viewpoints. It helps us to be extra
open-minded and willing to research from
others, recognizing that each individual
can offer a distinct point of view primarily
based on their special life story.

3. Promotes Inclusivity: Valuing man or
woman differences leads to more inclusive
environments, whether or not in non-
public relationships, workplaces, or
communities. It fosters an ecosystem
where humans feel valued and respected
for who they are, developing more
cohesive and supportive spaces.

4. Enhances Relationships: By recognizing and appreciating the specialty of each person, we can construct deeper, greater meaningful relationships. Understanding that everyone's wishes and ways of expressing love may additionally be exclusive allows us to tailor our interactions and construct stronger connections.

5. Inspires Personal Growth: Engaging with a numerous vary of folks exposes us to one-of-a-kind approaches of thinking and being. This can challenge our very own beliefs and assumptions, sparking personal increase and improvement as we learn from the forte of others.

6. Celebrates Individuality: Understanding

strong point promotes the social gathering of every person's individuality. This party encourages humans to categorical themselves authentically, enriching our lives and societies with their diverse talents, ideas, and cultures.

In essence, embracing the thinking of man or woman forte enriches our lives, deepening our connections with others and fostering a greater compassionate, open-minded, and inclusive world. It teaches us the fee of each and every human being and the beauty of our collective mosaic, composed of distinct and irreplaceable individuals. Indeed, appreciation and appreciating man or woman differences basically enrich our interactions and relationships in profound ways. This consciousness acts as a bridge, connecting us through our variety as a substitute than dividing us. Here are several key factors of how this appreciation can enhance our connections:

✓ Deepens Emotional Connections: By recognizing and valuing the unique preferences, needs, and feelings of others, we can tailor our strategy to give a boost to our emotional bonds. This personalized interaction fosters a deeper sense of intimacy and connection.

✓ Improves Communication: Understanding character variations helps us to talk more effectively. By recognizing how every character high-quality receives data and expresses themselves, we can regulate our verbal exchange style to improve appreciation and keep away from misunderstandings.

✓ Promotes Conflict Resolution: Awareness of unique views and problem-solving processes permits us to navigate conflicts extra constructively. Instead of clashing over differences, we can are seeking common floor and appreciate diverse solutions, turning viable conflicts into opportunities for growth.

✓ Increases Tolerance and Patience: Acknowledging that each character has their own set of challenges and strengths fosters persistence and tolerance. This attitude helps us to be more forgiving and supportive when others don't meet our expectations or when misunderstandings arise.

✓ Enhances Teamwork and Collaboration: In crew settings, whether or not in the place of work or social projects, valuing character variations can drastically raise teamwork and collaboration. By leveraging numerous skills, viewpoints, and approaches, organizations can acquire more innovative and positive outcomes.

✓ Cultivates Compassion: Understanding that anyone has a unique story crammed with their own struggles and triumphs nurtures a compassionate strategy to our interactions. This empathy encourages us to support every other in instances of need and have a good time our victories, fostering a sense of community.

✓ Encourages Personal Development: Engaging with humans who range from us can assignment our perspectives and spur personal growth. It pushes us out of our remedy zones and encourages us to advance a broader, extra inclusive view of the world.

By embracing individual differences, we not only enrich our very own lives but also contribute to a greater understanding, cohesive, and shiny society. This grasp for range strengthens our relationships, making our interactions greater meaningful and fulfilling. In a world that regularly emphasizes division, choosing to have fun and examine from our differences is a powerful act of solidarity and love.

Personality Traits To Cognitive Ability

The relationship between personality features and cognitive capability is a charming region of learn about that intertwines components of psychology and neuroscience. Being aware of how persona features relate to cognitive capabilities can help us apprehend person differences in learning, problem-solving, and creativity. Here's a concise exploration of this topic:

1. Openness to Experience:

- Relation to Cognitive Ability: Individuals excessive in openness to journey tend to show off sturdy creative questioning capabilities and possess a wide vary of interests. This trait has been linked to better overall performance on tasks that require divergent thinking (the ability to assume of many options to a problem).

- Impact: Such men and women are greater probably to engage in innovative and intellectual pursuits, which can in addition enhance cognitive flexibility and problem-solving skills.

2. Conscientiousness:

- Relation to Cognitive Ability: While conscientiousness is more about diligence, organization, and dependability than cognitive talent per SE, it positively influences tutorial and work performance. This trait supports a disciplined strategy to gaining knowledge of and problem-solving.

- Impact: High levels of conscientiousness can lead to better data retention, planning, and execution of complex tasks, indirectly pertaining to to cognitive processing efficiency.

3. Extraversion:

- Relation to Cognitive Ability: The hyperlink between extraversion and cognitive capability is now not straightforward. However, extraverts regularly excel in duties that require verbal exchange and social cognition, benefiting from their preference for social interactions.

- Impact: Their capacity to navigate social situations can beautify cognitive capabilities related to grasp and influencing others, though it may additionally now not at once replicate in usual measures of cognitive ability.

4. Agreeableness:

- Relation to Cognitive Ability: This trait is characterized by using compassion and cooperativeness. People with excessive ranges of agreeableness may operate better in tasks that require empathy and grasp of others' perspectives.

- Impact: While now not without delay

linked to prevalent cognitive ability, high agreeableness can make contributions to higher social cognition and collaborative problem-solving.

5. Neuroticism:

- Relation to Cognitive Ability: High ranges of neuroticism, characterised by using emotional instability and anxiety, can negatively have an effect on cognitive performance. This is frequently due to the truth that anxiousness and stress can impair memory, attention, and decision-making processes.

- Impact: Efforts to manipulate the bad components of neuroticism, such as via mindfulness or stress-reduction techniques, can help mitigate its influence on cognitive function.

Understanding the relationship between personality traits and cognitive skills can be in particular really useful in academic and occupational settings. Tailoring gaining knowledge of and working environments to suit person personalities can maximize productiveness and satisfaction. For instance, encouraging these excessive in openness to have interaction with innovative tasks, or making use of the organizational strengths of these who are conscientious, can lead to extra fine outcomes. Moreover, recognizing that positive characteristics would possibly influence cognitive competencies may want to motivate individuals to have interaction in practices that bolster their cognitive functions. Finally, this standpoint fosters a extra inclusive appreciation that cognitive competencies are multifaceted and influenced by using a complicated interaction of personality, environment, and biology. In sum, while personality characteristics are distinct from cognitive abilities, their relationship is intertwined in methods that drastically have an effect on how we learn, technique information, and interact with the world around us.

Improving cognitive abilities can be tailor-made to your personality traits, supplying a personalized and high quality approach.

Here are techniques aligned with a range of character dimensions:

1. Openness to Experience

- Embrace New Learnings: Engage in things to do outside your relief zone. This should be gaining knowledge of a new language, choosing up a musical instrument, or exploring new cultures via books and documentaries.

- Creative Exercises: Allocate time for creativity—painting, writing, or any shape of expression that encourages novel ideas.

2. Conscientiousness

- Structured Learning: Set clear goals for cognitive enchantment and create a structured diagram to reap them. This should include normal brain-training exercises, puzzles, and strategic video games like chess.

- Time Management Practices: Enhance cognitive feature through effective time management strategies, allowing for committed studying periods whilst warding off cognitive overload.

3. Extraversion

- Social Learning: Leverage your social nature by means of engaging in crew studying sessions, debates, and discussions. These interactions can beautify cognitive flexibility and verbal exchange skills.

- Active Environments: Study or work in dynamic, stimulating environments that healthy your energy levels, fostering concentration and productivity.

4. Agreeableness

- Collaborative Projects: Work on team-based tasks or volunteer things to do that require problem-solving and creative thinking, utilising your cooperative and empathetic nature.

- Mentorship: Either mentoring others or discovering a mentor for your self can raise cognitive skills through the trade of expertise and experiences.

5. Neuroticism

- Stress Management Techniques: Practice mindfulness, meditation, or yoga to decrease stress ranges and enhance awareness and memory retention.

- Positive Thinking Exercises: Cognitive-behavioural strategies that encourage nice questioning can assist manage the negative impacts of stress and nervousness on cognitive function.

Cross-Trait Strategies

Additionally, some techniques advantage most persona types, including:

- Physical Exercise: Regular bodily activity boosts brain fitness and cognitive feature regardless of personality.

- Healthy Diet: A balanced food regimen

rich in omega-3 fatty acids, antioxidants, and nutritional vitamins helps cognitive health.

- Adequate Sleep: Quality sleep is essential for memory consolidation and standard cognitive efficiency.

By aligning improvement techniques with your persona traits, you create a harmonious method to enhancing cognitive abilities. It's also really helpful to periodically reassess your strategies, as each your cognitive wants and personality can evolve over time.

Why Do The Difference Exist

Differences exist across various dimensions – be it in man or woman characteristics, cultures, beliefs, or experiences – due to a multitude of factors, ranging from evolutionary biology to sociocultural influences. Understanding why these differences exist requires exploring numerous key areas:

1. Biological Diversity: At a primary biological level, genetic variant is imperative to the survival and evolution of species. Genetic variations lead to

versions in traits, which can grant benefits in adapting to one of a kind environments. This version is no longer simply fundamental for individual survival however additionally for the resilience of populations and species as a whole.

2. Cultural Evolution: Cultures evolve primarily based on historical contexts, geographical locations, and social interactions. These evolutions result in a extensive range of languages, traditions, practices, and beliefs among one of a kind societies. Cultural differences are shaped via a myriad of factors which includes climate, herbal resources, historical events, and interactions with different cultures.

3. Psychological Differences: Individual variations in personality, intelligence, and different psychological characteristics are partly hereditary and partly fashioned by way of environment. Psychological theories, like those of Freud, Piaget, or Jung, emphasize distinct factors of personality improvement and cognitive growth, influenced by way of each innate factors and life experiences.

4. Societal and Economic Factors: Social structures, economic systems, and political ideologies also make contributions to differences amongst individuals and communities. These systems determine get entry to to resources, education, and opportunities, which in flip structure

individual and collective identities and capabilities.

5. Technological Progress: As communities boost technologically at specific charges and in a number of directions, technological disparities emerge. These differences can affect communication, healthcare, education, and universal high-quality of life, in addition diversifying human experiences and capabilities.

6. Historical Trajectories: The history of a region or group influences its present day nation significantly. Histories of colonialism, war, migration, and trade have left indelible marks on the identities, economies, and social constructions of

peoples, contributing to the rich tapestry of world diversity.

Understanding the motives behind differences is crucial for appreciating the complicated interaction of factors that form the human experience. It highlights the significance of context in decoding behaviours, beliefs, and abilities. Recognizing and valuing these variations is key to fostering inclusivity, empathy, and cooperation in a globally interconnected society.

Biological diversity, basically rooted in genetic variation, plays a pivotal function in shaping the variations among humans and populations, contributing to the prosperous tapestry of lifestyles on Earth.

This diversity encompasses the variants in physical traits, susceptibilities to diseases, and even behavioral tendencies, with its outcomes observable at both individual and populace levels. Understanding how this range arises and influences life necessitates a look into various key areas:

1. Genetic Variation: At the heart of organic range are the differences in the genetic make-up of organisms. These editions take place as a result of mutations, genetic recombination in the course of sexual reproduction, and gene waft throughout populations. Mutations introduce new genetic cloth into a gene pool, while recombination and gene float shuffle current genetic substances to create

new combinations. This genetic version is the raw fabric for evolution and is essential for a species' adaptability and survival.

2. Natural Selection: Natural decision acts on the range within a population, favouring traits that improve survival and reproductive success in a given environment. Over time, this leads to adjustments in the genetic makeup of populations, with recommended features becoming more common. This system can result in populations of the same species diverging genetically and phenotypically if they inhabit one-of-a-kind environments or have distinctive behaviours that have an

effect on survival and reproduction.

3. Speciation: As populations of a species grow to be greater genetically distinct, they might also subsequently grow to be separate species, a process recognised as speciation. This can happen thru geographic isolation, where populations are physically separated, or thru reproductive isolation, the place populations come to be genetically or behaviourally incompatible. Speciation provides to the biodiversity of an ecosystem, increasing the wide variety of species that can fill a variety of ecological niches.

4. Adaptation to Environments: Different environments exert distinctive selective

pressures, leading populations to evolve adaptations suitable to those conditions. For instance, populations living in high altitudes have diversifications for utilizing oxygen greater efficiently, whilst those in arctic climates might also evolve larger physique sizes to preserve heat. These variations contribute to the diversity considered within and amongst species.

• Genetic Drift*m: Apart from natural selection, genetic glide

— random adjustments in gene frequencies in a populace

— additionally contributes to diversity. In small populations, genetic go with the flow can lead to big changes over time, even if the adjustments do now not confer a survival advantage. This can enlarge variety amongst populations, in particular these that are isolated or have long gone via a bottleneck event.

• Disease Resistance and Susceptibility: Genetic diversity additionally influences the vulnerability of folks and populations to diseases. Different genetic versions can offer resistance or susceptibility to a number pathogens. This dynamic interplay between hosts and pathogens can lead to co-evolutionary races, the place each evolves new strategies to counter the other, similarly driving genetic diversity.

Biological diversity, ensuing from these genetic and evolutionary processes, ensures the resilience and adaptability of existence in the face of altering environments and challenges. It allows for a broader vary of responses to environmental change, reduces the risk of extinction from diseases, and underpins the complex ecosystems on which all life eventually depends.

Genetic drift is a key mechanism of evolutionary change and performs a essential function in shaping organic diversity. It refers to random modifications in the frequency of alleles (variations of a gene) within a population over time. These random changes can end result from a number of factors, along with populace size, founder effects, and population bottlenecks, every influencing biological diversity in unique ways.

✓ Population Size: In small populations, genetic waft can have a greater vast have an impact on because random occasions can substantially alter allele frequencies from one era to the next. Over time, this can lead to a minimize in genetic version within the population, as alleles can end up constant (where an allele's frequency becomes 1) or lost (where an allele's frequency will become 0) basically by chance. Conversely, in large populations, the impact of genetic flow is diluted as the threat of huge shifts in allele frequency due to random sampling is reduced, keeping genetic range to a greater extent.

✓ Founder Effect: This occurs when a new populace is mounted via a very small quantity of folks from a larger population. Since the founders characterize a small genetic sample of the authentic population, the new population may additionally have notably special allele frequencies. This can lead to decreased genetic range in the new populace if the founders carry a confined variety of alleles. The founder effect illustrates how genetic float can create new populations that are genetically distinct from their father or mother population, contributing to biological variety on a large scale.

✓ Population Bottlenecks: A bottleneck occurs when a massive populace experiences a sudden and substantial discount in size, frequently due to environmental events (natural disasters, unexpected climate changes) or human things to do (habitat destruction, overhunting). The survivors' genetic make-up largely determines the genetic range of the future population. Since the surviving group may not characterize the genetic diversity of the authentic population, the bottleneck can lead to a full-size loss of alleles, reducing genetic diversity. However, over long periods, populations that continue to exist bottlenecks can diverge genetically from their authentic populations, contributing to typical organic diversity.

Genetic drift influences biological range by using altering allele frequencies in populations, in particular small ones, in a directionless manner. While it can lead to a decrease in genetic range within populations via the loss of alleles, it additionally contributes to the diversity among populations by using creating genetically awesome businesses through strategies like the founder effect and populace bottlenecks. Understanding genetic float is fundamental for conservation efforts, as maintaining genetic range is necessary for the health, resilience, and adaptability of species.

CHAPTER 2

The Nature Of Individual Difference

The nature of man or woman difference lies in the appreciation that every man or woman is unique, with a awesome set of traits that differentiates them from others. This encompasses a wide vary of dimensions, together with however now not constrained to, personality traits, Genius levels, physical abilities, talents, preferences, emotional responses, and existence experiences. These variations occur from a complex interplay of genetic, environmental, cultural, and situational factors.

1. Genetic Factors: The genetic make-up

of an man or woman performs a imperative position in figuring out physical qualities such as height, eye color, and predisposition to positive fitness conditions. It can additionally have an effect on aspects of character and intelligence.

2.   Environmental Factors: The surroundings in which a character grows up and lives, inclusive of family dynamics, education, social interactions, and cultural background, appreciably shapes their beliefs, values, habits, and cognitive development.

3. Cultural and Societal Influences: Culture and society impart norms, values, and behaviors that affect an individual's

worldview, attitudes, and the way they interact with the world around them.

4. Personal Experiences: Individual experiences, which include traumas, achievements, relationships, and different giant lifestyles events, play a pivotal role in shaping one's identity, perspectives, and emotional resilience.

Understanding and appreciating these individual differences is necessary for developing inclusive communities, tailoring academic and occupational approaches, and fostering significant interpersonal relationships. Recognizing the special contribution of each character can lead to a greater empathetic, productive, and harmonious society.

Personal experiences appreciably contribute to shaping man or woman variations through influencing personality, beliefs, coping mechanisms, and emotional responses. These experiences, ranging from daily interactions to substantial life events, play a pivotal role in the development of an individual's persona and perspective. Here's an overview of how personal experiences structure man or woman differences:

1. Personality Development: Experiences in childhood, which includes the kind of parenting received, education, and social interactions, are foundational in creating character traits. For instance, kids who experience supportive parenting are

probable to improve self assurance and social competence, whilst these going through adversity may develop resilience or, conversely, emotional vulnerabilities.

2. Beliefs and Values: The cultural, social, and familial context within which an person grows up influences their trust structures and values. Personal experiences, such as travel, education, and engagement with numerous groups, can project or support these beliefs, main to a extensive spectrum of worldviews and values amongst individuals.

3. Coping Mechanisms and Resilience: The way folks react to and cope with challenges is closely influenced by their experiences. Those who have faced and

overcome adversity frequently enhance resilience and a set of coping mechanisms that can distinctly differ from those who have had less publicity to difficult situations.

4. Emotional and Psychological Impact: Experiences of trauma, loss, or good sized emotional activities can have profound effects on psychological well-being and emotional regulation. The processing and integration of these experiences into one's existence story can lead to extensive character differences in emotional responses, empathy, and psychological health.

5. Interpersonal Relationships: Personal experiences in relationships, whether tremendous or negative, impact social skills, attachment styles, trust, and the ability to shape and preserve relationships. Varied experiences lead to a large range of interpersonal behaviours and preferences amongst individuals.

6. Motivations and Goals: The lifestyles goals and motivations that power an man or woman are often shaped by means of their non-public experiences. Successes, failures, recognitions, and setbacks all play crucial roles in deciding one's aspirations, fears, and the paths they choose to pursue.

7. Cognitive and Moral Development:

Experiences that mission an individual's thinking, expose them to new ideas, or require moral decision-making contribute to cognitive complexity and moral reasoning abilities. Encounters with numerous views can significantly have an impact on the development of vital thinking and moral principles.

Understanding the affect of personal experiences on man or woman differences emphasizes the importance of empathy and personalised techniques in education, mental health, and social interactions. It highlights how a deep grasp of each person's unique trip can lead to extra high-quality communication, support, and cooperation in a variety of elements of life and society.

Leveraging the perception of private experiences to decorate intellectual fitness guide and interventions involves recognizing character differences, tailoring approaches, and fostering an surroundings of empathy and openness. Here are ways to use this grasp effectively:

1. Personalized Mental Health Care: Tailor intellectual fitness interventions to align with an individual's specific experiences, character traits, and cognitive patterns. Personalization could involve custom-made therapy sessions, targeted coping strategies, and interventions that resonate with the individual's existence

story and current challenges. Empathy and Validation: Cultivate empathy in therapeutic settings through validating personal experiences. This method helps build trust and rapport, making men and women feel understood and supported, which is indispensable for effective mental health support.

3. Cultural Sensitivity: Incorporate cultural competence into intellectual fitness practices to better apprehend and recognize diverse backgrounds and experiences. This fosters a greater inclusive and fine therapeutic environment.

4. Strength-Based Strategies: Identify and construct upon the individual's strengths

and resilience factors derived from their special experiences. Encourage practices that beautify these strengths as a skill of coping with intellectual fitness challenges.

5. Empowering Self-Understanding: Educate humans on the importance of introspection and self-awareness in grasp their own personalities and experiences. This know-how can empower them to be energetic individuals in their intellectual fitness journey, figuring out what works exceptional for them.

6. Community and Peer Support: Recognize the price of shared experiences in mental health support. Facilitate neighbourhood aid agencies or peer guide systems the place men and women can

exchange stories, strategies, and encouragement. Shared experiences can support a experience of understanding and belonging.

7. Technology and Personalization: Employ technology, like AI and computer learning, to analyse and predict the most high quality intervention strategies based on an individual's personality, behaviour, and trip patterns. This can lead to extra accurate and impactful intellectual fitness support.

8. Continuous Feedback Loop: Implement a mannequin of non-stop remarks the place humans can express how interventions have an impact on them personally. Use this feedback to regulate

and refine approaches, making sure they remain relevant and superb over time.

9. Educational Programs: Develop educational programs that train humans to appreciate character variations and understand how these differences affect mental health experiences and needs. This can promote broader societal support for personalized intellectual health interventions.

By deeply understanding and valuing non-public experiences, mental health experts can craft interventions that are not only extra advantageous but also extra compassionate. This strategy no longer solely improves mental fitness results however additionally contributes to a extra empathetic and grasp society as a whole.

Temperament

Human temperament refers to the basic, inborn personality features that have an impact on how a person behaves and interacts with the world. These features are considered to be biologically decided to a extensive extent and have a tendency to remain stable throughout an individual's lifespan. Temperament shapes how humans reply to their environment, control emotions, and set up patterns in social interactions. It's frequently described through a number dimensions such as:

1. Reactivity and Self-regulation: This includes how intensely humans respond to stimuli and their capacity to manipulate and modulate these responses.

2. Activity Level: The normal electricity degree in day by day activities, ranging from rather active to more sedentary behaviours.

3. Sociability and Approach/Withdrawal: This relates to how humans reply to new human beings or situations, from eager engagement to hesitation or avoidance.

4. Emotional Intensity: The energy of emotional responses, whether or not they're normally even-keeled or greater prone to excessive feelings.

Psychologists have proposed one of a kind fashions to categorize temperament. One of the most common is the three kinds suggested by way of Alexander Thomas and Stella Chess, which classifies teenagers as exceptionally being of "easy," "difficult," or "slow to heat up" temperaments primarily based on their regularity, adaptability, and responses to the environment. Understanding temperament is crucial in a variety of contexts, such as in academic settings the place procedures can be tailor-made to guide special learning styles, or in therapy, where insights into a person's temperament can inform greater advantageous coping strategies and therapeutic interventions. It's important to note that while temperament offers a foundational layer of personality, it does not predetermine a person's conduct or future; environmental factors, experiences, and mindful options play a sizeable position in shaping an individual's development and life path. Determining your own temperament includes self-reflection, observation, and now and again the use of structured tools or assessments. Here are some steps you can take to recognize your temperament better:

1. Self-Reflection: Start with the aid of reflecting on your reactions to quite a number situations. Consider how you typically reply to stress, change, or social interactions. Are you adaptable, or do you

locate alleviation in routine? How do you categorical and control emotions? Your natural inclinations in these areas can give you perception into your temperament.

2. Feedback from Others: Often, friends, household members, and colleagues can provide precious insights into elements of your personality that you may no longer absolutely recognize. They can provide perspectives on how you react below stress, your power tiers in extraordinary settings, and how you relate to others.

3. Journaling: Keeping a journal of your each day reactions to different occasions can be illuminating. Note any patterns in your behaviour, emotional responses, and idea processes. Over time, this can help

spotlight steady characteristics that factor to your underlying temperament.

4. Temperament Scales and Questionnaires: There are quite a few well-established temperament scales and questionnaires designed via psychologists to assist folks apprehend their temperament. Instruments like the Kersey Temperament Sorter, the Eysenck Personality Questionnaire, and the Clinger's Temperament and Character Inventory can grant structured feedback on distinctive aspects of your temperament. While some tools are available online, others can also require professional administration.

5. Consider the Context: Remember that behaviour can be context-dependent. You may respond one way in a acquainted placing and every other in a novel situation. Understanding the have an effect on of context can help make clear the nature of your temperament.

6. Comparison with Established Temperament Models: Familiarizing yourself with distinctive temperament models (e.g., the 4 temperaments theory, the Big Five personality traits, or the Thomas and Chess model) can provide a framework for perception your behaviours. Comparing your self-observations with these models may assist become aware of the place you suit within

these established categories.

7. Professional Guidance: For a greater comprehensive analysis, think about consulting a psychologist or a licensed counselor. They can provide professional assessments and interpret the results, imparting deeper insights into your temperament and how it interacts with a variety of factors of your life.

Determining your temperament isn't about pigeonholing your self into inflexible categories but perception the herbal dispositions that have an impact on how you perceive and have interaction with the world. This self-knowledge can be empowering, guiding private growth, enhancing relationships, and informing strategies to manage stress and challenges effectively.

Temperament refers to the simple inherited style of an individual's personality. It influences how they have interaction with the world around them, such as their behaviour, mood, and thinking patterns. Psychologists have recognized countless models to classify unique kinds of temperament. Here are some of the gorgeous ones:

1. The Four Temperaments

This is one of the oldest temperament theories, at the start proposed by way of the historic Greek doctor Hippocrates. It suggests that there are 4 indispensable persona types:

- Sanguine: Optimistic, social, and high-spirited however can be without problems distracted.

- Choleric: Ambitious, leader-like, and full of life but can be domineering.

- Melancholic: Thoughtful, considerate, and innovative however can be overly cautious or gloomy.

- Phlegmatic: Relaxed, peaceful, and quiet but can be shy and resistant to change.

2. Eysenck's Personality Inventory

Hans Eysenck proposed a mannequin based totally specially on genetics, emphasizing two foremost dimensions of temperament:

- Extraversion vs. Introversion: This dimension relates to the level of sociability and enthusiasm.

- Neuroticism vs. Stability: This dimension entails emotional steadiness and adaptability.

Eysenck later delivered a 1/3 dimension:

- Psychoticism vs. Socialization: This includes features such as aggressiveness and empathy.

3. The Big Five Personality Traits

Although now not a temperament mannequin per se, the Big Five persona features include factors thinking to have organic origins, akin to temperament:

- Openness: Creativity and a willingness to strive new things.

- Conscientiousness: A tendency to be equipped and dependable.

- Extraversion: An inclination toward being sociable and energetic.

- Agreeableness: A tendency to be compassionate and cooperative.

- Neuroticism: A tendency to experience poor thoughts like nervousness and depression.

4. Roth-Bart's Temperament Theory

Mary Roth-Bart's mannequin emphasizes

developmental aspects of temperament and identifies three primary dimensions:

- Extraversion: Generally entails impulsivity, pastime level, and looking for stimulation.

- Negative Affectivity: Tends to encompass fear, frustration, sadness, and discomfort.

- Effort Control: The ability to focus interest and exercise self-control.

5. Chess and Thomas' Classification

Stella Chess and Alexander Thomas recognized three basic types of temperament in their lookup on toddlers and children:

- Easy: Generally in a fine mood, ordinary in their organic rhythms, and adaptable to change.

- Difficult: Often in a negative mood, irregular in their biological rhythms, and tend to react intensely.

- Slow to Warm Up: Initially withdrawn or seemingly inactive, and they adapt slowly to new situations.

Each of these models highlights distinctive factors of temperament and its have an impact on persona development. It is vital to observe that character variations in temperament are thinking to be influenced through each genetic and environmental factors, suggesting a dynamic interaction in character development.

The Four Temperaments mannequin is an historic approach to understanding human personality, rooted in the traditions of Greco-Roman medicinal drug and philosophy. It suggests that there are 4 integral personality types: Sanguine, Phlegmatic, Choleric, and Melancholic. Each kind is related with a particular bodily fluid (humour) and well-known shows awesome characteristics and behaviours. This mannequin used to be in the beginning used via Hippocrates and later developed by way of Galen, a distinguished physician and philosopher, to understand health and disease and to provide hints for treating more than a few conditions.

1. Sanguine (Blood): Sanguine people are typically described as enthusiastic, active, and social. They tend to be outgoing, talkative, and at ease in social situations. Sanguine are regularly optimistic and have a excessive degree of energy, playing being concerned in things to do and attractive with others. However, they can every so often be distractible and trade their plans frequently.

2. Phlegmatic (Phlegm): Phlegmatic individuals are relaxed, peaceful, and quiet. They are stable, constant in their actions, and often excellent at mediation and bringing human beings together. Phlegmatic are considered as considerate

and caring, preferring steadiness and heading off conflict. They can, however, on occasion war with inertia and be resistant to change.

3. Choleric (Yellow Bile): Choleric human beings are leaders and dynamic individuals who are goal-oriented and have a lot of ambition and energy. They are frequently independent, decisive, and assertive. Choleric can be appropriate at planning and directing, however they would possibly sometimes be perceived as domineering or overly aggressive.

4. Melancholic (Black Bile): Melancholic individuals are frequently introspective, sensitive, and thoughtful. They can also have a deep grasp for splendor or art and

can be perfectionistic and detail-oriented. Melancholic are loyal and considerate, though they may additionally be inclined to fear and moodiness, often feeling things extra intensely than others.

The Four Temperaments model has mostly been outdated by present day psychological theories and fashions that are based on empirical research, such as the Big Five personality traits. However, the Four Temperaments continue to have an effect on our understanding of character in various contexts, including in some educational and therapeutic settings. The simplicity and intuitive appeal of the mannequin make it reachable for ordinary use, although it is vital to strategy it as a framework for understanding character as an alternative than a strict classification system.

Psychological Characteristics

Individual differences refer to the wonderful psychological characteristics that distinguish one character from another. These differences embody a vast array of features and attributes, which includes cognitive abilities, personality traits, emotional intelligence, motivations, and preferences. Understanding these distinctions is imperative for recognizing the unique ways in which human beings perceive, have interaction with, and respond to the world around them. Let's delve into some key areas:

1. Cognitive Abilities: Individuals differ notably in their cognitive capabilities, such as memory, attention, problem-solving skills, and the pace of processing information. For example, one character may excel in analytical thinking and logical problem-solving, while any other may have a strong spatial reasoning capacity or extraordinary creativity.

2. Personality Traits: The Big Five character model (openness, conscientiousness, extraversion, agreeableness, and neuroticism) presents a sturdy framework for exploring individual differences. For instance, an extraverted man or woman prospers on social

interactions, whereas an introverted individual may choose solitude and reflection.

3. Emotional Regulation and Intelligence: There are profound editions in how human beings understand, manage, and categorical their emotions. Some people are notably adept at recognizing and controlling their emotional responses, which enhances their capacity to navigate social conditions effectively.

4. Learning Styles: Individual variations are additionally obvious in mastering preferences and strategies. Some learners might benefit from visible aids and illustrations, others from auditory instructions, and but others from

kinesthetic or hands-on experiences.

5. Motivation and Goals: What motivates people can fluctuate greatly. Some are pushed with the aid of intrinsic elements like non-public growth, curiosity, or the joy of mastery. In contrast, others are stimulated by using extrinsic rewards such as money, recognition, or social status.

6. Resilience and Coping Mechanisms: People show gorgeous variability in their resilience—the capacity to bounce lower back from adversity. Likewise, coping strategies can differ, with some preferring problem-focused strategies to handle challenges head-on, while others might use emotion-focused tactics to manage their feelings about the problem.

7. Beliefs and Values: The beliefs and values humans hold shape their perceptions and moves in vital ways. These can have an impact on career choices, relationships, and even daily behaviour.

8. Interests and Preferences: From preferred entertainment things to do to profession interests, men and women vary broadly in what they find engaging, fulfilling, or enjoyable.

Recognizing and appreciating these man or woman differences is imperative for a range of applications, from designing extra high quality educational packages and work environments to fostering more healthy interpersonal relationships and growing greater tailor-made therapeutic interventions in medical psychology. It underscores the importance of a customized approach in many areas of existence and work, emphasizing the want to apprehend and appreciate every person's special psychological makeup.

CHAPTER 3

Genetics Foundation

The foundation of man or woman variations lies drastically inside genetics, shaping components of our personality, intelligence, and even predispositions to certain fitness conditions. Here's an overview of how genetics make a contribution to these variations:

1. Genetic Variation: Each character inherits a unique mixture of genes from their parents. These differences in genetic make-up are critical for the diversity in traits, abilities, and inclinations amongst individuals.

2. Personality and Behaviour: Studies on twins, in particular same and fraternal, have shown that genetics performs a sizeable position in character traits. For instance, extraversion and neuroticism exhibit a tremendous genetic influence. However, the surroundings also shapes how these features manifest.

3. Intelligence: Genetic elements make a contribution extraordinarily to versions in talent among individuals. Research suggests that 50-80% of the variability in talent (measured by IQ) throughout the populace can be attributed to genetic differences.

4. Physical Health: Genetics determine susceptibility to many diseases, which include diabetes, heart disease, and sure cancers. However, environmental factors and life-style options also drastically influence the onset and development of these diseases.

5. Mental Health: Similar to physical health, genetic predispositions play a role in the possibility of developing mental fitness disorders, such as depression, bipolar disorder, and schizophrenia. The interplay between genes and environmental stressors is crucial in the improvement of these conditions.

6. Gene-Environment Interactions: It's vital to understand that genetics does no

longer work in isolation. Genes have interaction with environmental factors, that means that a genetic predisposition may also solely turn out to be obvious or active underneath certain environmental conditions. For example, a character may have a genetic predisposition for high resilience, however this trait might also only grow to be evident when faced with large lifestyles stressors.

While genetics lay the groundwork for man or woman differences, the interplay between genes and the surroundings shapes the complexity of human characteristics. The learn about of epigenetics, which appears at how behaviours and environment can affect the way genes work, in addition emphasizes the dynamic interplay between our genetic makeup and our experiences. There is ongoing research in the area of genetics concerning intelligence. This region of study seeks to recognize how genetic elements contribute to variations in brain levels among individuals. The research integrates findings from more than a few disciplines, such as genetics, neuroscience, and psychology. Here are some key points related to modern-day research trends:

1. Genome-Wide Association Studies (GWAS): These studies contain scanning the genomes of many people to discover genetic variants associated with intelligence. Recent GWAS have

identified numerous genetic markers that appear to be linked to intelligence, though every marker has a very small effect. This suggests that intelligence is influenced through many genes, each contributing a tiny amount to the standard intelligence.

2. Polygenic Scores: Researchers are growing polygenic scores to predict intelligence the usage of facts from lots of genetic variants. These ratings estimate an individual's genetic predisposition to higher or lower intelligence. However, it's imperative to be aware that these predictions are probabilistic and no longer deterministic, as environmental elements additionally play a significant role.

3. Gene-Environment Interactions: Some studies are focused on understanding how genetic elements interact with environmental variables, such as education, socio-economic status, and nutrition, to impact intelligence. This line of research acknowledges that the expression of genetic doable for talent can be notably formed through the environment.

4. Ethical Considerations: As research advances, it raises vital ethical questions about privacy, genetic determinism, and the doable for social inequality. Scientists are also conscious of the historic misuse of intelligence lookup and are cautious to strategy the theme with rigor and

sensitivity.

5. Neurogenesis: This rising field combines neurobiology with genetics to discover how genetic editions have an effect on brain feature and structure, and thereby, cognitive abilities. Studies using talent imaging methods intention to hyperlink sure genetic profiles with patterns of talent connectivity that correlate with measures of intelligence.

Despite the progress, it is necessary to understand the complexity of brain as a trait. It is influenced by a great array of genes, environmental factors, and their interactions. Furthermore, brain is multidimensional, encompassing a range of cognitive abilities; therefore, shooting its genetic underpinnings remains a challenging task. The ongoing lookup is interesting and promising, but the full picture of how genetics have an impact on brain is nevertheless unfolding.

The Unique Combination Of Gene

The unique aggregate of genes that consequences in person differences—a cornerstone thinking in genetics—highlights the notable diversity within the human population. Each individual's genome is a distinct combo inherited from their parents, leading to a broad vary of physical, behavioural, and mental traits. Here's a simplified overview of how this genetic diversity contributes to person differences:

1. Genetic Variation: The human genome consists of about three billion base pairs of DNA. While over 99% of this DNA sequence is equal throughout all humans, the last fraction contains variants that make contributions to the variety in our physical appearance, susceptibility to diseases, and even behavioural traits. These variants consist of single nucleotide polymorphisms (SNPs), insertions, deletions, and different genetic alterations.

2. Alleles: Genes can exist in exceptional forms, acknowledged as alleles. Alleles contribute to the version in characteristics discovered among individuals. For

example, eye coloration is influenced by way of more than one genes, each with its own set of alleles ensuing in the spectrum of eye colorations considered in the human population.

3. Genetic Recombination and Mutation: During reproduction, genetic recombination and mutation introduce new genetic variations. Recombination happens when chromosomal segments are shuffled during the formation of sperm and egg cells, growing new combos of alleles. Mutations, which can take place spontaneously or due to environmental factors, introduce new genetic variants into the population.

4. Epigenetics: Apart from the DNA

sequence itself, man or woman differences are additionally influenced through epigenetics—modifications on top of DNA that affect gene expression without altering the genetic code. These changes can be influenced by way of lifestyle, environmental factors, and experiences, and in some cases, can be exceeded down to future generations.

5. Gene-Environment Interaction: The expression of genetic doable is notably influenced via environmental factors. For example, a individual may additionally have the genetic plausible for height, but terrible diet for the duration of childhood can forestall them from accomplishing this potential. Similarly, intellectual and

emotional improvement is formed via each genetic predispositions and experiences, such as education, social interactions, and culture.

These mechanisms underscore the profound complexity in the back of human diversity. It's no longer simply the genes themselves, but additionally how they engage with environmental factors, and even hazard activities for the duration of mobile phone division and development, that make contributions to the specialty of each individual. This biological tapestry ensures that even identical twins, who share the same DNA, can show off variations due to elements like epigenetics and man or woman lifestyles experiences.

Understanding the problematic dance between genes, environment, and risk continues to be a sizable research challenge, imparting insights not solely into human biology and behavior but additionally into customized remedy and the development of interventions that cater to individual genetic profiles.

The interplay between genes and surroundings in shaping man or woman differences is a complicated and dynamic process, often illustrated through the idea of gene-environment interaction (GxE). This interaction acknowledges that the outcomes of genes on more than a few traits, such as personality, intelligence, and susceptibility to disease, can be influenced, modified, or even induced with the aid of environmental factors. Here's a extra specific explanation:

1. Genetic Predispositions: Everyone inherits a unique set of genes from their parents, which includes versions that can predispose humans to positive qualities or behaviours. However, whether and how these genetic predispositions happen can rely significantly on environmental influences.

2. Environmental Factors: These include a vast vary of experiences and exposures in the course of a person's life, such as nutrition, education, stress, culture, and social interactions. Environments can enhance, inhibit, or alter the expression of

genetic potential.

3. Epigenetic: This is the find out about of how behaviours and surroundings can motive modifications that have an effect on the way your genes work. Unlike genetic changes, epigenetic adjustments are reversible and do now not exchange your DNA sequence, but they can trade how your body reads a DNA sequence. For instance, stress or vitamin can lead to epigenetic changes that have an effect on gene expression, doubtlessly influencing health and behaviour.

4. Examples of GxE:

- Intelligence and Education: A toddler with a genetic predisposition for high

Genius would possibly reach his doable in a stimulating surroundings with access to academic resources. Conversely, a lack of these resources might obstruct mental development no matter the genetic potential.

- Personality: Genes have an effect on persona traits, however how these qualities are expressed can be substantially affected by using lifestyles experiences. For example, a genetically predisposed resilience may additionally be nurtured thru supportive relationships and challenges.

- Mental Health: Genetic vulnerabilities to mental health issues like depression or nervousness can be exacerbated or mitigated by way of environmental factors such as stress, trauma, or aid systems.

5.   Moderation and Mediation: Environment can average the impact of genes (changing the power or path of a genetic impact based totally on distinct environmental contexts) and mediate genetic consequences (acting as an middleman mechanism through which genetic predispositions lead to outcomes).

Understanding gene-environment interactions is integral for appreciating the complexity of human development and person differences. It underscores the significance of thinking about both genetic and environmental factors in addressing health, educational, and psychological issues. This knowledge also helps the development of customized interventions that can more successfully promote well-being by way of taking into account an individual's unique genetic make-up and environmental context.

CHAPTER 4

Environmental Influences

Environmental influences play a quintessential position in shaping individual differences in personality, intelligence, abilities, and fitness outcomes, complementing genetic factors in finding out who we become. These influences range widely, from the prenatal environment, which encompasses exposure to nutrients and toxins in the womb, to the broader, lifelong experiences such as education, culture, social interactions, and even unintended occurrences.

1. Early Life Experiences: The experiences we have in our early years, along with the fantastic of care, attachment styles, early education, and social interactions, substantially influence our cognitive and emotional development. For instance, enriched environments with enough instructional assets can beautify cognitive abilities, while adverse experiences like overlook can hinder psychological development.

2. Socioeconomic Status (SES): SES encompasses income, education, and occupational status, and it profoundly influences man or woman differences. Higher SES regularly presents get entry to to better instructional opportunities,

healthcare, and social networks, fostering cognitive improvement and basic health. Conversely, lower SES is associated with elevated exposure to stressors, which can adversely affect intellectual and bodily health.

3. Education: Education is a integral environmental issue that influences cognitive abilities, understanding acquisition, and even personality features like conscientiousness. The fantastic and quantity of schooling can drastically affect character differences in intelligence and different cognitive abilities.

4. Culture and Social Environment: The cultural context influences values, norms, behaviours, and even the manifestation of

certain personality traits. For example, collectivist cultures might prioritize community and family over man or woman achievements, affecting the development of private identification and interpersonal relationships.

5. Nutrition and Health: Nutrition, specifically in quintessential developmental periods, has a profound have an impact on on cognitive development and physical health. Malnutrition can lead to long-term cognitive deficits, whilst a balanced weight loss program supports highest quality intelligence development and functionality.

6. Life Experiences and Learning: Unique experiences, along with travel, hobbies, and occupations, make contributions to individual variations via shaping interests, knowledge, and skills. Lifelong gaining knowledge of and publicity to numerous views foster cognitive flexibility and creativity.

7. Technology and Media: In the digital age, technological know-how and media are considerable environmental influences, affecting attention, information processing, social interactions, and even sleep patterns. The content material and period of publicity to screens can have different influences on cognitive and social development.

It's necessary to understand the dynamic interaction between genetics and the environment, acknowledged as gene-environment interaction. Traits and skills are now not solely determined by genetic predispositions or environmental factors; rather, how genes specific themselves can be influenced via the environment. This interaction underscores the complexity of individual differences, highlighting that our improvement is a continuous procedure shaped by using each our organic makeup and the myriad experiences we come across all through life.

Socioeconomic fame (SES) plays a pivotal position in shaping individual differences, impacting cognitive abilities, persona traits, and standard health outcomes. This impact is multifaceted, encompassing get right of entry to resources, educational opportunities, and environmental stressors.

1. Education and Cognitive Abilities: SES is closely linked to academic opportunities. Higher SES frequently affords get right of entry to to higher best education, stimulating cognitive development and improving capabilities such as problem-solving, memory, and verbal abilities. Moreover, families with greater SES are more in all likelihood to make investments in educational tools and extracurricular activities, similarly advertising cognitive growth.

2. Health Outcomes: There is a robust correlation between SES and health. Higher SES persons commonly have better access to healthcare services, more healthy diets, and safer residing environments. This can lead to reduced exposure to fitness dangers and persistent stressors, which are acknowledged to negatively affect cognitive functions and general health.

3. Stress and Mental Health: SES influences exposure to stress and its management. Chronic stress related with decrease SES, such as monetary instability and unsafe neighbourhoods, can have an effect on mental health, main to improved danger of melancholy and anxiety. These

stipulations can avert cognitive overall performance and social functioning.

4. Nutrition and Physical Development: Nutritional great varies considerably with SES. Poor diet can have an effect on early intelligence improvement and cognitive abilities, as properly as bodily health. Higher SES is often related with diets that aid most useful intelligence characteristic and development.

5. Social and Cultural Capital: The assets handy through a family's social networks, often tied to SES, can provide additional opportunities for development and success. This includes access to information, assist systems, and influential social circles that can open doors to

instructional and career opportunities.

6. Environmental Quality: Higher SES frequently permits families to stay in safer, cleaner neighbourhoods with better access to parks and recreational facilities. These environmental factors contribute to bodily well-being and cognitive development thru greater opportunities for physical recreation and much less publicity to environmental toxins.

7. Language Development: Children from greater SES households are regularly uncovered to a richer language environment, with more substantial vocabularies and complex sentence structures. This fosters early language improvement and literacy skills, which are

imperative for educational success and fantastic communication.

Socioeconomic popularity is a quintessential determinant of individual differences, affecting a extensive array of results from cognitive competencies and fitness to character development. The impact of SES highlights the importance of addressing social inequalities to enhance developmental potentials across populations.

Environmental Factors

Environmental elements play a pivotal function in shaping character variations amongst people, interacting intricately with genetic predispositions to make contributions to the forte of every individual. These factors embody a vast vary of influences that individuals are exposed to at some point of their lives, from pre-natal stipulations to cultural and socio-economic backgrounds. Here is an overview of key environmental factors affecting character differences:

1. Early Life Conditions: The prerequisites an person is exposed to prenatally and all

through early childhood can have long-lasting effects. Nutritional status, publicity to toxins, and maternal stress degrees for the duration of pregnancy can have an impact on developmental outcomes. Early childhood experiences, along with nurturing, publicity to language, and physical care, appreciably influence cognitive and emotional development.

2. Education and Learning Opportunities: Access to schooling and the best of instructional experiences play critical roles in shaping cognitive abilities, social skills, and knowledge bases. Opportunities for gaining knowledge of and engagement in intellectually stimulating activities contribute to individual variations in

intelligence, creativity, and problem-solving skills.

3.   Socioeconomic Status (SES): Socioeconomic factors, along with income, occupation, and instructional attainment of one's family, can have an effect on get admission to assets like nice education, nutritious food, and healthcare. SES influences stress levels, dwelling conditions, and ordinary well-being, which in flip influence cognitive development and fitness outcomes.

4. Cultural Influences: Culture shapes beliefs, values, behaviours, and language. It influences persona traits, cognitive styles, and social interactions. For instance, individualistic cultures may

foster independence and self-expression, whilst collectivist cultures might emphasize community and familial ties.

5. Social Relationships: Interactions with family, friends, and broader social networks affect emotional development, self-esteem, and interpersonal skills. Supportive relationships can promote resilience and well-being, while negative social experiences, such as bullying or social isolation, can negatively have an effect on intellectual fitness and personal development.

6. Physical Environment: The satisfactory of one's physical environment, together with dwelling conditions, exposure to pollution, and get right of entry to to green

spaces, can have an effect on health and well-being. Urban versus rural living prerequisites also offer special units of opportunities and challenges, influencing life-style and activities.

7. Life Experiences: Personal experiences, together with travel, work, adversity, and amusement activities, make a contribution to a person's knowledge, skills, values, and worldview. Traumatic activities might also result in psychological changes, whilst high quality experiences can foster growth and resilience.

The interaction between these environmental factors and genetics highlights the complexity of human development and man or woman differences. Understanding the function of the environment is indispensable in developing interventions and policies aimed at advertising greatest development and lowering inequalities.

Genetics As Blueprint

Genetics serve as a blueprint for character differences, laying the foundational underpinnings from which our unique characteristics emerge. Every human being inherits a set of genes from their parents, which interact in complicated approaches to determine our physical attributes, predispositions to certain fitness conditions, and even components of our persona and cognitive abilities.

1. Physical Characteristics: The most seen expressions of genetic have an impact on include bodily attributes like height, eye colour, hair colour, and facial features. These characteristics are without delay influenced by using the genetic facts handed down from our ancestors.

2. Health and Diseases: Genetics also play a imperative position in susceptibility to sure illnesses and conditions. For instance, particular genetic markers can extend the possibility of growing conditions such as coronary heart disease, diabetes, Alzheimer's, and certain cancers. However, it's important to observe that environment and lifestyle preferences can drastically have an effect on these outcomes as well.

3. Cognitive Abilities: Research suggests that genetics contributes to versions in cognitive competencies such as IQ, memory, studying ability, and problem-solving skills. Twin studies, in particular, have highlighted the genetic affect on

intelligence and cognitive diversity.

4. Personality and Behaviour: Genetics also impacts our temperament, susceptibility to intellectual fitness conditions, and factors of our personality. Studies of twins and adoptees provide proof for the genetic basis of features such as extraversion, neuroticism, and openness.

It's necessary to understand that whilst genetics grant the blueprint, the surroundings in which an man or woman is raised and lives plays a sizeable role in how these genetic potentials are realized. The interaction between genes and environment, often referred to as gene-environment interaction, shapes the improvement of person variations in a dynamic and ongoing process. For example, a genetic predisposition to excessive intelligence might only entirely happen with the guide of a stimulating environment, prosperous in academic opportunities.

Understanding the genetic blueprint of character variations is a unexpectedly evolving field, with advances in genomics and biotechnology presenting deeper insights into the complex net of factors that contribute to our uniqueness. However, it is additionally important to approach the subject matter with sensitivity to moral concerns and the practicable for misuse of genetic information.

CHAPTER 5

Embracing Diversity And Differences

Embracing range and variations in people entails recognizing, celebrating, and valuing the special traits and views each character brings. It goes beyond tolerance to create a lifestyle of acceptance, respect, and grasp for various backgrounds. Organizations gain from various perspectives that lead to innovation, creativity, and better problem-solving. By fostering inclusivity, understanding, and tolerance, men and women sense accepted, valued, and engaged, improving productivity and worker morale. Strategies like open conversations, inclusive leadership, and empathy are necessary in embracing diversity in the workplace. Teaching teenagers tolerance and acceptance from a young age is essential, starting at home and strengthened by way of educators. Celebrating range thru cultural events, education, and inclusive environments promotes harmony and a sense of belonging for all individuals. Ultimately, embracing variety is a journey that requires continuous effort, commitment, and a willingness to research from and respect the variations that make every man or woman unique.

Embracing diversity benefits humans and agencies in a range of ways. For individuals, it fosters inclusivity, understanding, and tolerance, leading to personal growth, open-mindedness, and a sense of unity. Diversity permits people to experience one of a kind perspectives, enriching their lives and advertising appreciate for unique traits and backgrounds. In the workplace, embracing range leads to a broader talent pool, increased worker happiness, higher patron loyalty, higher communication, and increased productivity. Diverse teams are extra innovative, creative, and better at problem-solving due to the range of experiences and views they bring. Organizations that prioritize variety and inclusion ride higher income growth, higher readiness to innovate, expanded capability to recruit pinnacle talent, and substantially greater worker retention rates. Ultimately, embracing diversity advantages men and women via creating a more inclusive surroundings the place all and sundry feels valued and revered while benefiting businesses through superior creativity, innovation, productivity, and competitiveness.

Organizations can measure the impact of diversity initiatives via various quantitative and qualitative metrics. Quantitative measurements focus on factors like representation, hiring practices, pay equity, merchandising rates, turnover, and accessibility of programs and services. By inspecting these metrics, organizations can check the alignment of their staff with diversity benchmarks and identify areas for improvement in recruitment, development, and retention strategies. Qualitative measurements, on the different hand, listen on consequences such as employee inclusion, purchaser feedback, and engagement with worker useful resource groups. These measures provide insights into the perceived stage of inclusion felt with the aid of employees and the effectiveness of range efforts in recruiting, retention, and training. Additionally, assessing leadership commitment, company-level metrics like applicant pool vs. hires and company-wide range distribution, as properly as the use of data-driven procedures through surveys and center of attention groups can help companies evaluate the success of their diversity initiatives. Regular evaluations, soliciting employee feedback, and conducting impact assessments are critical steps to continually improve and refine variety initiatives based totally on measurable outcomes.